# SCHIRMER'S LIBRARY
## OF MUSICAL CLASSICS

# SONATA ALBUM
## Twenty-Six Favorite Sonatas
## For the Piano

By

## HAYDN, MOZART, and BEETHOVEN

Edited, Revised, and Fingered by
SIGMUND LEBERT, HANS von BÜLOW
AND OTHERS

IN TWO BOOKS

→ Book I: 15 SONATAS — Library Volume 329

Book II: 11 SONATAS — Library Volume 340

ISBN 978-0-7935-2577-5

# G. SCHIRMER, Inc.

DISTRIBUTED BY

HAL•LEONARD®
CORPORATION
7777 W. BLUEMOUND RD. P.O. BOX 13819 MILWAUKEE, WI 53213

# Contents

## Book I

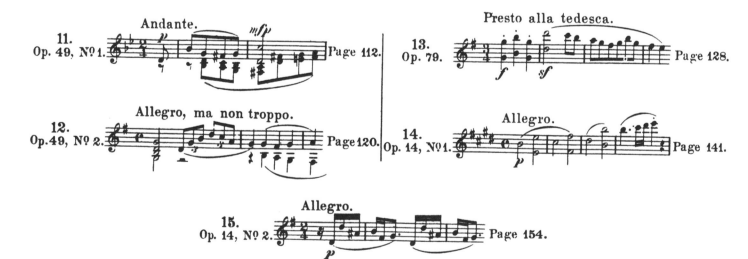

# Contents
## Book II

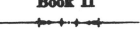

## Haydn

## Mozart

## Beethoven

# SONATA.

Abbreviations: M. T. signifies Main Theme; Ep., Episode; S.T., Sub-Theme; Cl. T., Closing Theme; D. G., Development-group; Md. T., Mid-Theme; R., Return; Tr., Transition; Cod., Codetta; I, II, III, signify 1st, 2nd, and 3rd parts of a movement in song-form (Liedform.)

Allegro con brio. (♩ = 96.)

JOSEPH HAYDN.

11699 r

a) The short turn in small notes is intended for inexpert players. In the original, these turns are all marked thus:

Printed in the U. S. A.

4

11699

a) ![easier notation] easier: ![easier notation]    b) After the hold a fairly long pause should be made.

a) Sustain the hold, and then proceed without interruption.

6

a) This hold is longer than the preceding one; before continuing, a fairly long pause should be made.

a) Inexpert players may omit the first note of each turn, as before.
b) The hold sustained, and followed by a brief pause.

8

11699

a) Duly subordinate the accompaniment. b) [music example] easier: [music example]

c) Strike all the tones of the chord in succession, from the lowest to the highest, and connect the preceding b with the high c.

**Finale.**
Allegro. (♩. = 63.)

# SONATA.

Allegro con brio. ($\bullet$ = 116)

JOSEPH HAYDN.

14

a) In the original, mordents are given here; but inverted mordents are doubtless intended.
b) After the hold, a slight pause should be made.

11705

**Menuetto.** ( ♩ = 108.)

a) These turns alwoys fall on the last note of the accompaniment-figure; in this case, therefore, on the third note of the second beat.
b) Continue without further pause.

11705

Trio.

Menuetto D.C.

a) b) c) As at b).

**Theme.**

Presto. (♩ = 152.)

**Var. I.**

**Var. II.**

11705

# SONATA.

Abbreviations: M.T. signifies Main Theme; Ep., Episode; S.T., Sub-Theme; Cl.T., Closing Theme; D.G., Development-group; Md.T., Mid Theme; R., Return; Tr., Transition; Cod., Codetta; I and II, 1st and 2nd parts of a movement in song-form (Liedform.)

Allegro con brio. (♩ = 138.)

JOSEPH HAYDN.

*) In view of the rapid tempo, only an inverted mordent, consisting of 3 equal notes, accenting the first, can well be played:

11701 r x

a)

**Largo e sostenuto.** (♪ = 69.)

a) Strike the tones in succession, from the lowest to the highest, and hold all down.

b) As above.

## Finale.

Presto, ma non troppo. ($\bullet$ = 144.)

a) This accompaniment-figure must be kept duly subordinate to the melody.  b) [image] easier [image]

11701

# SONATA.

Abbreviations: M.T. signifies Main Theme; Ep., Episode; S.T., Sub-Theme; Cl.T., Closing Theme; D.G., Development-Group; Md.T., Mid-Theme; R., Return; Tr., Transition; Cod., Codetta; I, II, III, signify 1st, 2nd, and 3rd parts of a movement in song-form (Liedform.)

JOSEPH HAYDN.

Moderato. ($\textit{♩} = 92.$)

*) In this motive the sign ∾ does not signify a turn with the ordinary division ▬▬▬, but serves as an abbreviation for the figure: ▬▬▬ which, in analogy with the initial motive, must be imitated throughout the movement in all similar situations.

11700 r

11700

**Scherzando.**

Allegro con brio. (♩ = 120.)

**Menuetto.**
Moderato. (♩ = 132.)

a) [figure] b) Commence with the principal note, as at a). c) As above.

11700

# SONATA.

Abbreviations: M. T., signifies Main Theme; Ep., Episode; S. T., Sub-Theme; Cl. T., Closing Theme; D. G., Development-group; Md. T., Mid-Theme; R., Return; Tr. Transition; Cod., Codetta; I, II, and III, 1st, 2nd, and 3rd parts of a movement in song-form (Lied-form.)

JOSEPH HAYDN.

a) After the hold a considerable pause should be made.

11696

a) After the hold, a brief pause should be made.

42

a) Duly subordinate the accompaniment.

b) In rapid tempo, the turn between two notes of this value may best be executed as follows:

11696

a) After the hold, make a brief pause.

a) Continue after a short pause.

# SONATA I

W. A. MOZART

Abbreviations: P. T., Principal Theme; S.T., Secondary Theme; Close; D., Development; Coda; M.T., Middle Theme.

Abkürzungen: HS. bedeutet Hauptsatz. SS. Seitensatz, SchlS. Schlusssatz, DS. Durchführungssatz. Anh. Anhang, MS. Mittelsatz.

a) *mp (mezzo piano)* rather soft; viz., between *p* and *mf*

a) *mp (mezzo piano*, ziemlich schwach) bedeutet einen Grad von Tonstärke, welcher zwischen *p* und *mf* steht.

b)  Less skillful players may content themselves with the following execution:  or: 

Schwächere Spieler können sich mit folgender Ausführung begnügen: or even with an inverted mordent.

oder auch mit einem Pralltriller.

11134

48

11134

# Rondo
## Allegretto grazioso (♩ = 104)

# SONATA IV.

Abbreviations, etc.: P. T., Principal Theme; S.T., Secondary Theme; Close; M. T., Middle Theme.

Abkürzungen: HS. bedeutet Hauptsatz, SS. Seitensatz, SchS. Schlusssatz, MS. Mittelsatz.

a) Strike the a with the chord in the bass.

a) Das a muss gleichzeitig mit dem Accord im Basse eintreten.

b)     c)     d)     e)     for less skilled players.
für schwächere Spieler:

a) Strike these appoggiaturas with the accompaniment.

b)  for less skilled players.
für schwächere Spieler:

a) Diese Vorschläge gleichzeitig mit der Begleitung anzuschlagen.

58

11137

11137

Allegretto. (♩ = 104.)

P.T. HS.

a)  *mp* (*mezzo piano*) rather soft; viz., between *p* and *mf*

a)  *mp* (*mezzo piano, ziemlich schwach*) bedeutet einen Grad von Tonstärke, welcher zwischen *p* und *mf* steht.

11137

# SONATA VII.

**Abbreviations, etc.: P. T., Principal Theme; Ep., Episode; S. T., Secondary Theme; Close; M. T., Middle Theme; T., Transition; Coda; D., Development.**

**Abkürzungen: HS. bedeutet Hauptsatz, ZwS. Zwischensatz, SS. Seitensatz, SchlS. Schlusssatz, MS. Mittelsatz, ÜG. Uebergang, Anh. Anhang, DS. Durchführungssatz.**

a) In this movement, the bass-notes provided with pressure-marks should be sustained during the three following eighths, as if half notes.

b)

a) Die mit diesem Dehnungszeichen versehenen Bassnoten in dem vorliegenden Satze werden am besten noch während der drei folgenden Achtel (also wie die halben Noten) ausgehalten.

*poco marcato.*

a) Begin the appoggiatures in both hands exactly up-on the beat, and strike the principal notes together also.

b)

11140

a) Die Vorschlagsnoten müssen in beiden Händen gleichzeitig, und zwar genau auf den Taktstrich, an-fangen, sowie hernach auch die Hauptnoten zusammen anzuschlagen sind.

Close. SchlS.

a)

11140

a) The following suffices
for less skilled players:

b) As at b., on the next page.

c) As at a.)

a) Für schwächere Spieler genügt:

b) wie bei b) auf nächster Seite.

c) Ausführung wie bei a.)

Allegro assai. (♪= 96.)

a) *mp* (*mezzo piano*) rather soft; viz., between *p* and *mf*.

a) *mp* (*mezzo piano*, ziemlich schwach) bedeutet einen Grad von Tonstärke, welcher zwischen *p* und *mf* steht.

b)

Close. SchlS.

11140

11140

11140

11140

Coda. Anh.

# SONATA.

W. A. MOZART.

11135

84

11135

a) Notes marked with a line (–) in this edition, should be played rather heavily (pressed out.)

b)

c) To be rendered as at b.

a) Die mit (–) bezeichneten Noten sind hier und an den ähnlichen Stellen etwas gewichtig anzuspielen.

c) wie b) auszuführen.

11135

a) easier:
leichter:

a) Begin the trill with the principal note.

a) Den Triller mit der Hauptnote beginnen.

90

a)

Close.
SchlS.

a)

11135

**CODA.**

a) Execute the arpeggiated chords swiftly, the hands attacking and quitting them exactly together.

a) Die Arpeggien dieser letzten zwei Accorde müssen in beiden Händen gleichzeitig anfangen und aufhören, und rasch ausgeführt werden.

# SONATA IX.

Abbreviations: P.T., Principal Theme; S.T., Secondary Theme.

Abkürzungen: HS. bedeutet Hauptsatz, SS. Seitensatz.

**Tema.**

Andante grazioso. (♪ = 120.)

**Var. I.**

a) *mp* (*mezzo piano*, rather soft,) viz., between *p* and *mf*.

a) *mp* (*mezzo piano*, ziemlich schwach) bedeutet einen Grad von Tonstärke, welcher zwischen *p* und *mf* steht.

a)

**Var. II.**

a) ![easier figure] easier:
leichter:

b) Strike these appoggiaturas exactly on the beat.

c) ![easier figure] easier:
leichter:

b) Die Vorschlagsnote mit dem *cis* oben gleichzeitig anschlagen, und so fort.

Var. III.(♪ = 112.)

sempre legato.

### Var. V.
Adagio.(♪ = 60.)

a) See a), previous page.
c) Wie a) auf voriger Seite.

Begin the embellishment with the bassnote *a*, and execute it so quickly, that the principal note—*c sharp*, is struck before the entrance of the *c sharp* in the bass.

Den Vorschlag mit dem *a* im Basse zu beginnen, jedoch so schnell auszuführen, dass die Hauptnote *cis* noch vor dem *cis* des Basses eintritt.

**Var. VI.**

Allegro. (♩ = 116.)

a) Make these appoggiaturas very short, but distinct; strike them exactly on the beat.

b) The *c* sharp must enter with the fundamental note of the left hand. All the broken chords in this variation are very emphatic.

c)

d) Both hands begin and end together.

a) Diese Vorschläge auf den Anfang des Takttheils, sehr kurz aber deutlich.

b) Mit der Grundnote der linken Hand muss das *cis* in der rechten Hand eintreten. Alle gebrochenen Accorde in dieser Variation sehr markirt.

c)

d) Beide Hände zusammen anfangen und aufhören.

11142

a) Play the first note of the embellishment with the bass.

a) Die erste Vorschlagsnote tritt gleichzeitig mit dem Bass ein.

a)

b) This trill is undoubtedly intended to end with the following figure in thirty second notes, instead of the usual turn: . But the customary close is easier, and is allowable:

b) Dieser Triller ist wohl ohne den gewöhnlichen Nachschlag von unten beabsichtigt, indem die folgenden Zweiunddreissigstel die Stelle des letzteren vertreten: Zur Erleichterung mag jedoch folgende Ausführung gewählt werden:

Trio.

a) The appoggiaturas on the beats. | a) Die Vorschläge auf den Anfang des Takttheils.

11142

Menuetto D.C.

# Rondo

**Alla Turca**

Allegretto (♩ = 126)

W. A. MOZART

a) Always begin the embellishment on the beat.

b) 

c) Play the bass with the c sharp in the right hand, accent it strongly, and so proceed throughout the entire theme.

a) Den Vorschlag immer mit dem Takttheil beginnen.

c) Der. Bass muss mit dem cis der rechten Hand gleichzeitig eintreten und sehr markirt gespielt werden, auf gleiche Weise durch den ganzen Satz.

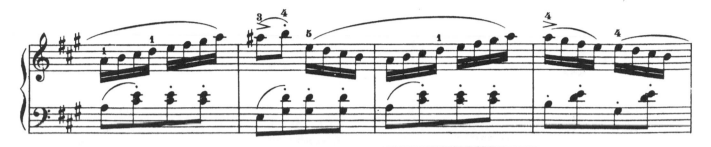

a) Sustain the half note c sharp, but otherwise play the chords alike in both hands. Let the hands begin exactly together, and attack the highest note together.

b)  c) The appoggiaturas as at **b.**

a) Die Ausführung in der rechten Hand ist wie in der linken Hand, nur dass die halbe Note cis gehalten wird; rechte und linke Hand muss gleichzeitig beginnen und gleichzeitig auf dem obersten Ton eintreffen.

b) c) Ausführung des Vorschlags wie bei **b.**

# Two Easy Sonatas, Op. 49
## No. 1, in G minor

Abbreviations: M. T., signifies Main Theme; S. T., Sub Theme; Cl. T., Closing Theme; D. G., Development-group; R., Return; Tr., Transition; Md. T., Mid-Theme; Ep., Episode; App., Appendix.

L. van BEETHOVEN.

a) *mfp* signifies: the first note *mf*, the following ones *p*.

b) With the comma we indicate places where the player must perceptibly mark the end of a rhythmic group or section, by lifting the last note just before its time-value expires, although the composer wrote no rest.

c)

d) The left hand more subdued than the right, but still accenting the first of each pair of 16th-notes (i. e.: the bass notes proper) somewhat more than the second.

e)

f) Here and in the next measure the left hand should accent only the first note in each group of 16th-notes somewhat more than the others, but in all cases less than the soprano.

g) As at d.)

h) In these three measures as at f.)

a) As at (f) on the preceding Page.

b) 

c) The left hand here again more subdued than the right.

d) As at (a).

e) In these twelve measures the first and third notes in each group of 16th notes should be made somewhat more prominent than the other notes, yet always in subordination to the melody, excepting the tones marked >.

11622

**f)**

**a)**  From here through the next 6 measures the left hand, having the melody, should predominate over the right and, where it has 2 tones, chiefly accentuate the higher one.

**b)**  As on first Page.

**c)**  The next 5 measures as on first Page.

**d)**  Doubtless literally meant neither for ♪♪♪♪♪ nor for: ♪♪♪♪♪ but ♪♪♪♪♪

**e)**  This and the following turns again as on first Page.

**f)**  From here onward as on second Page.

### Rondo.
Allegro. (♩. = 92.)

a)

b) Proceed only after a rest.

.a) In these groups of 16th - notes, accent each first note slightly more than the 5 following, while subor-
dinating all to the soprano. These same accented notes, too, (except in the fourth measure) should be held
down during the second 16th-note.

b) Also subordinate this accompaniment, but accent the first note of each triplet, as the bass note proper,
a trifle more than the other two.

a)

b) Here, of course, only the first eighth-note in each measure should be accented.

a) From here up to the **ff** discreetly subordinate the left hand throughout (also in the repetitions of the fundamental tone.)

b) Let the **ff** enter abruptly with the fourth eighth-note, without any previous *crescendo*.

# Two easy Sonatas.

## Op.49, № 2.

Abbreviations: M.T. signifies Main Theme; S.T., Sub-Theme; Cl. T., Closing Theme; D.G., Development-Group; R., Return; Tr., Transition; Md. T. Mid-Theme; Ep., Episode.

L. van BEETHOVEN.

**Allegro ma non troppo.** (♩ = 132.)

a) Strike all short appoggiaturas on the beat, simultaneously with the accompaniment-note.

b) F♯ should be executed as a long, accented appoggiatura:

11628

a) easier:

11623

a) *mp* (*mezzo piano*, moderately soft) signifies a degree of tone-power midway between *p* and *mf*.

# SONATA.
## Op. 79.

L. van BEETHOVEN.

a) It is interesting to observe how much more genius, i. e.: virility (yet without prejudice to its grace.) Beethoven exhibits in his treatment of the characteristic local note of his Viennese environment (the "Landler,") when in the mood for employing it, than does Franz Schubert. The affinity of this "alla tedesca" to the Intermezzo of like name in the grand String-quartet Op. 130, is also worthy of note:

b) Avoid all useless time-beating with the left hand, but mark the anticipation of the dominant harmony on the third beat, which, as a peculiarity of the Master's later style, assures the connoisseur of Beethoven with greater reliability than any antiquarian researches, that this Sonatina is no "Jugendarbeit" (youthful work.)

11628ᵣ

a) The animated waltz-rhythm, in which the third beat also has a slight accent, must be brought out equally in both hands.

b) This trill is to be conceived simply as an inverted mordent with after-beat (quintuplet), and begun on the principal note.

a) The seemingly inconvenient fingering given by the Editor serves to urge the right hand to greater agility and an increase of sonority resulting therefrom; and also
b) to prevent collision with the superposed fingers of the left hand.

131

**a)** Here, as on the preceding page, the Editor has taken the liberty of giving a different shading to promote animation in the 4-measure period, by whose frequent repetition indifference is far too easily induced. If the first 3 measures (tonic) are played *piano*, the fourth (dominant) may take an accent, in order to distinguish it from the 3 first measures of the after-phrase (dominant); the same holds good in the other case, where, by omitting in the fourth measure the *sforzato* given in the first three, the former is negatively emphasized.

**b)** The thematic "stretto" requires that, instead of playing 4 measures in $\frac{3}{4}$ time, 6 measures should as it were be played in $\frac{2}{4}$ time, thus obtaining a grateful variety of effect.

**c)** This inverted slide is executed simply thus: the rapid movement not admitting of its treatment as a turn.

a) This waltz, like the celebrated waltz in Weber's "Freischütz," must be executed *pianissimo* and with no retardation whatever; a slight acceleration in tempo is admissible.

a) This movement may be regarded as the prototype of the modern "Song without Words", and one hardly surpassed in amiable and original freshness by any.

Imagine the first subject executed by wind-instruments — say clarinets and bassoons; one measure before the second subject, the muted strings fall in, while oboe and flute alternately bear the melody.

b) The profuseness in the directions for the fingering is justified by our experience, that no player executes with finish pieces of such apparently easy technique until he recognizes them to be "difficult!" The change of fingers expressly called for in places like  is indispensable for the special reason, that the "vis inertiæ" of the fingers often causes, in execution, mistaken ideas as

to the leading of the parts

a) As the passage ascends *crescendo,* the quintuplet is to be played:

b) The *sforzato* indubitably refers to the second 16th-note E♭, not to the third ($^c_a$), where it would sound coarse and tasteless; its sharpness must, moreover, be mitigated by a preceding increase in power accompanied by a moderate *ritardando.*

a) As implied by the term "Schneller" (inverted mordent; lit. a "snap") it is well to execute this grace with a change of fingers conducive to a snap:

b) The Editor divides this passage between the hands, and therefore lets the right hand lead off:

a) All efforts toward an exact mathematical proportioning of the accompaniment-triplets to the duple rhythm of the theme, will be vain. Only assiduous separate practice with each hand will lead to the requisite independence. Compare Note (a) on Page 131 (Op. 54), where the method for practice is discussed.

a) This measure must have the character of an interrogation. The answer, with the re-entrance of the theme, must follow as naïvely as possible.

b) The short appoggiaturas must also be included in the value of the principal note, not figuring as auftakts, but thus:

# 141
# SONATA.
### Op. 14. No 1.

To Baroness von BRAUN.

Abbreviations: M. T. signifies Main Theme; S. T., Sub-Theme; Cl.T., Closing Theme; D. G., Development-group; R., Return;
Tr., Transition; Md. T., Mid-Theme; Ep., Episode.

L. van BEETHOVEN.

a) *mp* (*mezzo piano*, somewhat soft) indicates a degree of power between *p* and *mf*

b)

c) To be held a full quarter-note.

d) Emphasize the *forte* and *piano* sharply, and accent the first notes of the *piano* only gently.

e) This appoggiatura is to be executed within the duration of the second quarter-note, so that the E of the 3d quarter-
note falls exactly on the 3d beat:

Copyright, 1894, by G. Schirmer, Inc.
Copyright renewal assigned, 1923, to G. Schirmer, Inc.
Printed in the U.S.A.

11612r

11612

a) The slurs over the soprano, both here and in the parallel passage further on, are undoubtedly set wrongly, and ought to connect only the second quarter-note with the following half-note; hence a fresh attack is to be made with F♯ and D♯ in the two highest parts, (as with A♯ in the third part), which we have indicated by the dot under the slur and over the first quarter-note.

a) In this *decrescendo*, too, the highest part should predominate slightly over the accompanying notes.

11612

a) This tenor part should be so distinctly brought out, as to betoken its derivation from the principal motive.

a) See Footnote b) on Second Page.

a) By a comma we indicate rhythmical divisions or groups, which the player must make perceptible, although they are not indicated in the composition by means of rests.

11612

Maggiore.

Coda.

# Rondo.

**Allegro commodo.** ($\d = 76$)

11612

**a)** The *staccato*-mark over the first note of each triplet signifies, as often happens in Beethoven (and in earlier times still more commonly), not a *staccato*, but a stronger accentuation of the respective notes.

**b)** Carefully observe this abrupt *piano*.

a) The bass, which here takes up the principal motive (in the variant appearing immediately before in the right hand), should be played with peculiar stress.

# SONATA.
## Op.14, Nº 2.

154

To Baroness von BRAUN.

Abbreviations: M. T. signifies Main Theme; S. T., Sub-Theme; Cl. T., Closing Theme; D. G., Development-group; R., Return; Tr., Transition; Md. T., Mid-Theme; Ep., Episode.

L. van BEETHOVEN.

11613x

a) Execute the entire figure delicately, but with such accentuation that its rhythmic position in the measure shall be distinctly defined.

b)      c)

a) Properly subordinate the inner part.

b) Keep all these syncopated notes well subordinated. c)  easier:  or thus:

11613

a Properly subordinate inner part.

162

Andante. (♩ = 76.)
*La prima parte senza replica.*
Tema.

Var. I.

a) *mp sempre legato.*

a) *mp* (*mezzo piano*, moderately soft) denotes a degree of power intermediate between *p* and *mf*. In this whole Variation (excepting the 4 closing measures) the principal melody, which lies in the inner part (in the higher inner part in the first measure after the repeat), must distinctly sound as such.

11613

a) The melody-notes which we have distinguished by specially marking them as eighth-notes or quarter-notes, must not merely be held as such, but gently emphasized; the first and last notes, in each of these figures consisting of 3 16th-notes, must be most subordinated —— even more so than the bass part.

b) *Rinforzando* signifies here, as is often the case, a stronger emphasis not only of a single note, but of a whole passage.

## Scherzo.

Allegro assai. (♩. = 76.)

a) The three notes of this motive should be kept cleanly and distinctly apart throughout, while plainly marking their rhythmic position in the measure by proper (but never rough) accentuation, thus:

11613

a) This mere accompaniment should be more subdued than the higher part; the later sustained notes should, to be sure, be somewhat emphasized, but always in subordination to the melody

a) Do not retard.